D1179130

S
7

JN 04309706

LINCOLNSHIRE COUNTY COUNCIL	
04309706	
PETERS	£10.99
02-Oct-07	941.081

Real Lives

Victorian Country Children

Four real children, four different lives

Sallie Purkis

Contents

A & C Black • London

Life in the countryside

When Victoria became Queen in 1837 most families in Britain lived in the countryside. They lived in small villages where everyone knew everyone else. They were all christened and married in the village church or chapel, and they would eventually be buried there. Landowners, farmers and the vicar had big houses. Other people lived in small cottages. There was one main street with a pub, a shop and workshops where things were made or repaired. They included a blacksmith's forge where horses were fitted with new horseshoes.

Once a week a carrier came into the village, bringing packages and parcels. Most villages had a school, although children did not have to attend until a law was passed in 1871.

The richest and most important person in the village was the squire, who owned all the land and most of the cottages. The squire could turn families out of their cottages if they disagreed with him or if they were sacked from their jobs. In late August, after everyone had worked hard to get in the corn, the squire laid on a big feast for the whole village, called Harvest Home.

Life in the countryside was hard, particularly for those with little money. Most people lived without piped water, electric lights or heating. Families were much larger than they are today and children often had to share a bed with several brothers and sisters. People without money or a home, or those who were too old to work, had to go into a workhouse.

Rich people lived very differently. Landowners and their families lived in big country houses and employed people from the village to run their house for them. Their servants did almost everything, so they never had to learn to cook for themselves.

During Queen Victoria's long reign there were many changes in the countryside. Some farmers bought new steam-powered machines to do

Butleigh High Street, Somerset.

jobs on the farm. As a result, many people lost their jobs. Thousands of families became destitute and emigrated to Canada, Australia or America to begin a new life.

Some landowners sold part of their land to railway companies. Noisy, smoky steam engines soon rushed through fields that had once been quiet and peaceful. The railways began to carry coal and raw materials to the factories. This took jobs away from the families who worked on canal boats.

By the time Queen Victoria died in 1901, more people lived in towns and cities where they could find better houses and jobs than in a village.

In this book you can read about five children who lived in the countryside in Victorian times. None of them were famous. They all lived in the reign of Queen Victoria, but their lives were very different. Some went to school, some did not. Only the rich twins lived in a house that their parents owned. They also had servants to look after them. Boys and girls were treated differently, too, in Victorian times.

The stories of their lives have been put together from different sources of information. You can read about these on pages 4 and 5.

Walter lived in Somerset and was the son of a farm labourer. By the time he was nine he was working for the squire.

Richard's family lived on a boat on the Leeds to Liverpool Canal. He never stayed anywhere long enough to go to school.

Sarah and her sister were very poor. They had to live in a workhouse, on the edge of a village called Linton.

Tommy and Eva were twins who lived in a large country house in Cornwall. Their father was a very wealthy man.

LEEDS

LIVERPOOL

LINTON

BUTLEIGH

BODMIN

How we know

A biography is the story of someone's life written by another person. A biographer can use many different sources of information to write the story. These are some of the sources we have used to find out about the lives of the five children in this book.

Census returns

A census is taken every ten years and shows the names of everyone living in the country on census night. The information is kept private for 100 years, but we have been able to look at the forms for all the families in this book, including the Drapers who lived on a boat. The forms tell us how old the people were when the census was taken and where they were born.

Newspaper reports

We found the information about Sarah's trip to the seaside in a copy of an old newspaper. News about Tommy and Eva often appeared in the local newspaper because their father was wealthy and important.

LINTON.—*Workhouse Children's Treat.*—On Tuesday last, the children of the Union Workhouse enjoyed a delightful day at Harwich. Arriving at the sea-side about 10·30, they amused themselves by catching crabs and examining such "wonders of the deep" as sea-weeds, shells, &c. They then partook of a hearty luncheon, after which boats were engaged and a splendid voyage taken to the forts, which, with the cannon, &c., were examined very minutely; after a refreshing bathe, all returned to Harwich. Here all partook of a plentiful tea, and then commenced a merry homeward journey. The Great Eastern Railway Company, and others interested, are sincerely thanked for the liberal subscriptions received; and to Mrs. Howlett, great credit is due, for the excellent sandwiches, plum cakes, buns, &c.

Family letters

When Tommy and Eva's family gave their house, Lanhydrock, to the National Trust, they also left many boxes of letters. There are copies of some of them in the family museum, which is open to the public.

Old maps

Nineteenth century Ordnance Survey maps show us what villages were like when the maps were drawn.

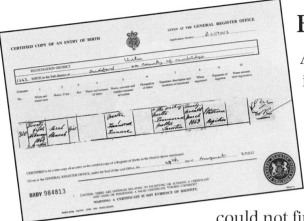

Birth certificates

A copy of everyone's birth certificate is kept in the Family Records Centre in London or the Register House in Edinburgh. These tell us when and where people were born and the names of their parents. This is a copy of Sarah's birth certificate. We could not find any certificates for Richard, who lived on the canal. Boat families never stayed in one place for very long, so Richard's parents may not have registered his birth.

Old photographs

Many towns have collections of old photographs in their libraries, archives or museums. Some museums use copies of photos, blown up, as part of their displays.

Directories

Every village was listed in a county directory. These can still be seen in the Record Office or Local Studies Libraries. They tell us the names of the landowners, farmers, shopkeepers and craftsmen who lived in villages.

Parish church and records

Look for monuments to rich people inside a local church. You may also find a list of vicars from the past. The inscriptions on graves in churchyards can help you to build up a picture of families from the names and dates on the stones. Children who were baptised in church have their names entered in the parish records. Nowadays, most of these records can be seen in a County or Borough Records Office.

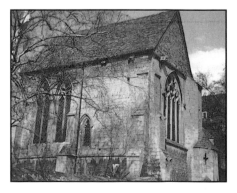

Richard

R ichard's family lived on a boat on the Leeds to Liverpool Canal. The boat took coal from the coal fields to textile factories. Richard's job was to look after the horse which pulled the boat along.

Richard Draper was born in 1878 in Lancashire, and grew up living on board a narrow boat with his parents, his older sister Mary Jane and his baby brother James. They never stayed long in one place. We only know about them because they were found by a man taking the census when their boat, *The Jupiter*, was moored at Shipley in West Yorkshire.

The Jupiter did not belong to the Drapers but to the Leeds to Liverpool Canal Company. The Drapers were employed to ply up and down the canal, carrying coal to the clothmaking

factories along the banks. The coal was used to fire steam engines that drove the machines that made wool and cotton cloth. In Victorian times, Yorkshire was famous for its woollen cloth and Lancashire for its cotton, so there were many factories needing a constant supply of coal.

The trip from Leeds to Liverpool was 127 miles long. Richard and his family passed through beautiful countryside as well as famous textile towns like Burnley and Blackburn, and the coal fields at Wigan. They also crossed the Pennine Hills, sometimes called the 'backbone' of England.

Many locks had been built along the canal route to help boats climb up and down hills. When *The Jupiter* entered a lock the water level had to be raised or lowered depending on whether the canal was going up or downhill. Richard helped his father work 21 locks. There were also two long, dark tunnels, and aqueducts (bridges for the canal) above small towns and villages.

The Jupiter was long and narrow, only about 24 metres by 5 metres, and was pulled along by a horse. Beside its name the words 'Leeds to Liverpool Canal Company' were painted together with a licence number. This number was used by lock keepers to check that a toll was paid every time the boat passed through a lock or a tunnel.

It must have been very cramped on board *The Jupiter*. Much of the space inside the boat was taken up with the cargo of coal.

The family ate and slept in one cabin where there was an open-fronted iron stove. The family used this for cooking, and for warming up and drying off after being outside in the cold or wet. Richard, Mary Jane and James could stand up in the cabin, but their mum and dad had to stoop because there was only a metre between the ceiling and the floor.

The cabin was cleverly designed to make the most of every scrap of space. All the furniture was built-in as part of the boat. Pots and pans, table and beds fitted into tiny shelves and cupboards. Everything had to be put away after it was used to leave a bit of room for the family to move around. At night Richard's parents slept in one big bed with baby James. Richard and his sister slept in two small beds that dropped down out of cupboards.

This picture shows a canal boat family eating together. You can see how little space they have.

The family did not own many clothes, which was a good job as there was nowhere to put them. Richard's father always wore a pair of corduroy trousers, a waistcoat, a striped, collarless shirt and a flat cap, which the Canal Company supplied. His mother wore a woollen dress, a bonnet, an apron and a warm shawl. Richard had to make do with clothes passed on from other children or made from scraps of his parents' old clothes. Most boat women were very good at crochet, which they used to decorate their clothes and brighten up the inside of the boat.

This boy is leading a horse along a towpath, just as Richard would have done.

It must have been very difficult for Richard's mother to keep anything clean on a coal boat that had no bathroom.

Drinking water came from a special barrel on deck and meals were simple. Most of the time the family made do with vegetable stew. If they could catch a rabbit or a duck, it was added to the pot. In autumn, the children collected wild berries, mushrooms and nuts, which were free. They were able to buy bread and milk from small shops that had grown up along the canal bank to supply boat families, like the Drapers.

Boat children worked hard from a young age, and as Richard grew up, he helped his parents more and more. Richard and Mary Jane's main job was looking after the family's horse. The horse walked along a path beside the canal, called the towpath, and pulled the boat along. It was important to keep the horse's oats dry and to collect sweet grass or hay for him in the fields, as most of the grass on the towpath was worn away. Whenever the boat stopped at a lock or tunnel, Richard and Mary Jane had to untie the horse and lead him around to the other side. From time to time they came across stables that the Leeds to Liverpool Canal Company had built. Richard would give the horse a quick nosebag and a little rest overnight. Caring for the horse was a big responsibility because if the horse became ill, the family could not continue their journey and earn their living.

As they were always on the move, Richard could not go to school. However he learnt many things as he travelled up and down the canal. He knew the names of all the animals and birds he saw as the boat moved along. He recognised wild plants and flowers and knew which berries were good to eat and which ones were poisonous. He could also tell what the weather would be like the next day from looking at the clouds and the sunsets.

When Richard grew up

Richard learnt about boats from his parents so that he could take charge of a Company Boat himself one day. By the time he was grown up, many of the pulling horses had been replaced by steam tugs. These could tow three or four boats at a time, so it would have been harder for Richard to get work.

Sarah

Sarah had a mother and sister, but no father. Her little family had no money and no home, so Sarah spent her childhood in the workhouse, where life was hard.

Martha Townsend had a job as a nursemaid, helping to look after the children of a rich family who lived in Sawston, Cambridgeshire. She earned little money and worked long hours, but she lived in her employer's house and had a secure job. That all changed when Martha was only 19 and found out that she was pregnant. This news was a big problem. Martha was not married and in Martha's day people thought it was a disgrace to have a baby without first getting married.

Martha gave birth to a daughter in February 1863 and called her Sarah. After the birth Martha went straight back to her job. We do not know who looked after baby Sarah.

Sarah's mother could not read or write. On Sarah's birth certificate she just drew a cross. Underneath, the registrar wrote, 'The mark of Martha Townsend, mother'.

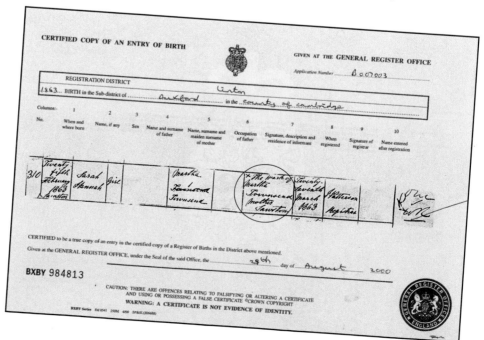

12

She may have been left with her grandmother, who had more children of her own.

We do not know who Sarah's father was because his name was not written on her birth certificate. Perhaps he already had a wife. We will never know as the information was kept secret.

Three years later, Sarah had a new baby sister, Jane, even though her mum had still not married. With two children under the age of four, Sarah's mother could no longer do her job and her grandmother probably did not have enough room or money to keep three extra people. So Martha, Sarah and baby Jane had to go and live in the workhouse.

People like Sarah and her family, who had nothing and nowhere to turn to, were called paupers. In the nineteenth century, unlike today, there were no benefits to help families manage when they were out of work. Instead, there was the workhouse. Here, they had to work very hard in return for somewhere to sleep, clothes and food. They were not paid any money for their work.

The Townsends went to a workhouse which was 10 miles from Sawston at a place called Linton. It was right on the edge of the village, apart from any other buildings.

Buses and cars didn't exist then so Martha
and her daughters had to walk, or they may have
asked for a ride on a passing farm cart.

It must have been very frightening for Sarah as she
walked through the workhouse entrance. It was the largest
building she had ever seen, built of red brick and rocks
of flint, collected from the fields nearby. The workhouse
staff took Sarah's clothes and made her change into the
workhouse uniform – a rough plain dress, woollen
stockings and a bonnet to keep her hair back.

Sarah had to quickly get used to her new daily routine, which rarely changed. She had to get up at 5.45 am in the summer and 6.45 am in the winter. She was given dry bread and a bowl of porridge, called gruel, for breakfast and then she went to the workhouse schoolroom for three hours of lessons. Sarah's mother may have looked after the babies. Some women worked in the kitchen preparing meals or in the laundry doing the washing.

Dinner was in the middle of the day. Sarah, Jane and their mother sat together to eat potatoes with a little meat. Then, in the afternoon, Sarah had various jobs. Sometimes she would help in the farmyard or fields that belonged to the workhouse or she did cleaning jobs, like scrubbing the stone floors.

In the evening there was more bread and homemade soup. Sarah's diet looks boring but she had better meals than many other poor people at that time. Finally it was time for bed. Sarah slept in a dormitory in a bed that she shared with her baby sister.

This girl is collecting water. Sarah had to do jobs like this at the workhouse.

The workhouse was managed by a committee called the Board of Guardians. It included important local people like farmers and the vicar. They met every month to make sure the finances were in order and to appoint the staff who ran the workhouse. They wanted life for the paupers to be hard as most Victorians thought that it was a crime to be poor.

This photograph is from The National Trust Workhouse at Southwell. It shows what Sarah's dormitory may have looked like.

15

Railway Station, Linton.

Sarah travelled on a train from Linton Railway Station when she went to the seaside.

There were nearly 200 people in the workhouse altogether. They all had to follow very strict rules. They could not go out of the workhouse without the permission of the Master and on every Sunday all the paupers had to attend chapel. Sarah attended the special Sunday School for the children.

Just occasionally, there were some special treats. At Christmas time, the Board of Guardians paid for a Christmas dinner of roast beef, plum pudding and a glass of beer for the grown-ups.

In August 1873 the children were taken for a day at the seaside. First the children all walked the mile and a half to Linton Railway Station and took the train to Harwich, where they arrived at 10.30 am. Sarah and the rest of the children were allowed to run around on the beach before eating a picnic lunch.

LINTON.—*Workhouse Children's Treat.*—On Tuesday last, the children of the Union Workhouse enjoyed a delightful day at Harwich. Arriving at the sea-side about 10-30, they amused themselves by catching crabs and examining such "wonders of the deep" as sea-weeds, shells, &c. They then partook of a hearty luncheon, after which boats were engaged and a splendid voyage taken to the forts, which, with the cannon, &c., were examined very minutely; after a refreshing bathe, all returned to Harwich. Here all partook of a plentiful tea, and then commenced a merry homeward journey. The Great Eastern Railway Company, and others interested, are sincerely thanked for the liberal subscriptions received; and to Mrs. Howlett, great credit is due, for the excellent sandwiches, plum cakes, buns, &c.

This is a copy of the original newspaper article that described Sarah's day at the seaside.

In the afternoon, they were taken for a boat trip to see an old fort with cannons that had been built in case of an invasion. When the tide came in they had a swim and a picnic tea of sandwiches and cakes before walking back to the station for their return journey to Linton.

A newspaper reporter wrote about the day for his paper. In the report he thanked the kind ladies of Linton who had collected money and prepared the food for the workhouse children.

When Sarah grew up

We have very little information about Sarah after 1871. We know that her family were no longer living in the workhouse when the census was taken in 1881. It is likely that at the age of nine Sarah became a servant in someone's house, just as her mother had been.

Tommy and Eva

Tommy and Eva were twins and their parents were very rich. They lived in a large country house, which had a nursery wing just for the children.

Twins Tommy and Eva were born on 22nd May 1880. Eva came first and Tommy twenty minutes later. The twins' full names were Julia Caroline Everilda Agar-Robartes and Thomas Charles Reginald Agar-Robartes. No wonder they were always called Tommy and Eva for short!

Their parents were very wealthy. Their father was a Lord's son and a Member of Parliament. They already had an older sister called Maye.

The twins were born at their parents' home in London. The nursery was all ready for their arrival. Brand new clothes were bought for them and two servants, a nanny and a nursemaid, were hired to look after them.

Their parents sent news of the twin's arrival by telegram to friends and family, including Tommy and Eva's grandparents who lived in Lanhydrock, a large country house in Cornwall. This is where their family had lived for over 250 years. After visiting the twins, their grandparents wrote letters saying that the twins were the most beautiful children they had ever seen.

A year later, some terrible news reached London in a telegram. Lanhydrock was on fire! Tommy and Eva's father left London at once. When he arrived, only one wing of the beautiful old house was still standing. Lady Robartes, aged 68, had only escaped by climbing down a ladder from an upstairs window and three days later she died from shock. Lord Robartes never properly recovered either and died the following year. This left Tommy and Eva's father the owner of an almost ruined country house.

He decided there was only one thing to do. He would move the family to Lanhydrock, but first they must rebuild the house with the best and most modern conveniences that money could buy. It took three years to finish, but everyone agreed that the new house was perfect.

The new kitchens were up-to-date and efficient, with special rooms to prepare the vegetables, cook bread and cakes, make cheese and clotted cream and store dry goods, fish and meat. There was a dining room, a smoking room for men only, a billiards room, a morning room which caught the early morning sun, a drawing room, a music room and a prayer room, as well as three staircases and bedrooms for the family and their staff.

After the fire destroyed Lanhydrock, Tommy and Eva's father had the kitchens rebuilt. You can visit the house and see them for yourself.

The whole family, including Tommy, Eva, their big sister Maye, younger brother Gerald and a tiny new baby called John, moved into the new house in the summer of 1884.

Everyone was happy in the new home, but tragedy struck on Christmas Eve. Baby John suddenly became ill and died, putting a stop to all celebrations. In the years that followed three more brothers and two sisters were born – making a total of nine children.

Tommy and Eva lived upstairs in the nursery wing with their younger brothers and sisters. The nursery wing was a whole corridor of rooms just for the children, including their own bathroom.

Nanny Coad was in charge with two nursemaids, Emma Rogers and Clara Hodge. The staff always had to call the twins Master Tommy and Miss Eva. Meals were sent upstairs from the big kitchen and milk from the dairy was put on the windowsill in a churn to keep it cool. Eva and Tommy had matching cots in the night nursery until they were big enough for a bed. In the day nursery they ate their meals and played with their toys. They even had their own schoolroom, with their own teacher who taught them to read and write.

Although they were twins (and Eva was the oldest), Eva and Tommy were treated differently once they were toddlers.

Tommy had a train set,
a fort and lead toy soldiers.
Eva played with her dolls'
house and made pretend pastries
and buns with her pastry set.
Eva's family praised her for her
singing and embroidery. Tommy was
admired for his horseriding and archery.

When it was fine, they went outside
to look at the horses in the stables, at the
coaches in the coach house and at the
Lanhydrock Fire Engine. The Home Farm
was a short walk away, so they went to
see the farm animals and collect eggs
from the hens' nesting boxes. The twins
each had their own pony. They had
learnt to ride in the park around the
house when they were five years old.

Tommy and Eva had
their portrait painted
with Gerald and Maye.

21

Every morning Tommy, Eva and all the other children went downstairs and joined the rest of the household in the prayer room to listen to readings from the Bible and join in prayers. On Sundays they went to the church next door to their house. Here they sat apart from everyone else in a special family pew.

At seven years old, Tommy was sent away from home to a boarding school in Reading. He only came home during the school holidays. As for Eva, a new governess arrived to teach her at home. The governess came from a musical family and taught Eva to play the piano and to speak French.

Every January, Eva's mother and the new governess organised a family concert. Eva played the piano while Tommy made everyone laugh with his funny songs.

After Tommy went to school, Eva began to go out with her mother to support good causes and charities, but it was always Tommy who was invited to open a new building. This is an example of the way boys and girls were treated differently in Victorian times.

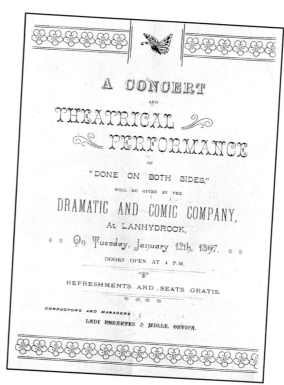

This is a programme from one of the twins' concerts.

When Eva grew up

Eva never went to school or college. After her mother died she ran the house, where she lived until she died in 1969. She worked with many charities. During the Second World War we know that she helped 17 evacuees from London and organised games, plays and concerts for them.

When Tommy grew up

Tommy went to Eton and Oxford University and then joined an army regiment called the Coldstream Guards. He became the youngest Member of Parliament in the House of Commons. He was killed in 1915 in the First World War at the Battle of Loos.

Walter

Walter lived with his family in the village of Butleigh. Their cottage was owned by the squire. Walter's family was poor and Walter had to work from a very young age.

Walter Hodges was born in 1852 in the village of Butleigh, near Glastonbury in Somerset. His parents, John and Rachel, had both lived in Butleigh all their lives and Walter was their first child. Their tiny cottage belonged to the village squire, George Neville Grenville, who also owned most of the farms around. His house, called Butleigh Court, was the only big house in the village.

Walter was born in the cottage. When Rachel felt the baby coming, she sent for the village midwife who brought a supply of clean rags to the house and busied herself with boiling water in the big pot hanging over the fire. This was the only way to heat water as there was no electricity or gas in the cottage. Even the water had to be collected from a pump down the street.

When Walter gave his first cry, the midwife bathed him and dressed him in baby clothes from a box sent round by the vicar's wife. Later, the clothes would have to be washed and put back

Butleigh High Street in 1900.

24

into the box for another mother to borrow. Walter didn't have a cot. He was probably put to sleep in a basket or a drawer.

When Walter was one year old, his mother had another baby, whom his parents called Catherine. Soon after, she gave birth to another boy called Thomas.

The cottage was crowded. There were two floors, but there was probably only one room downstairs and one room upstairs. Downstairs was for eating and keeping warm by the fire. When it grew dark the whole family went to bed upstairs. Walter had to sleep in the same bed with his brother and sister. The toilet was in a small shed at the bottom of the garden. It was called an earth closet and was shared by all the families in the row. There was no water to flush it clean. The contents had to be covered up with earth.

Walter's father was a farm labourer, but his mother did not have a regular job like her husband. She grew vegetables in the garden, kept chickens and a pig. She also had a beehive in the garden.

Sometimes Walter's mother walked to the nearest small town to collect work she could do at home. At harvest time she went out into the fields and earned a bit of money by helping to bring in the corn.

When Walter was old enough, he worked in the fields alongside his mother. Once the corn had been cut, Walter helped to collect the ears that had been left by the reaper. He and his mother were allowed to take these home for the family to eat. In winter he collected firewood for his mother or he was paid by the farmer to pick up stones from the fields. When the first shoots of wheat and barley began to grow, Walter was paid to scare off the birds. This was a job he had to do again when the corn began to ripen.

Every August was shooting season. The farmer paid Walter and other boys to go out tapping trees on the edge of the woods. This stopped the pheasants flying away, so the squire and his friends could shoot them. At the end of the shoot, the gamekeeper's wife gave the boys a meal of rabbit stew.

The job Walter always liked best was leading the farmer's horses from their stable onto the fields and holding them still while the men loaded the farm cart.

Walter's father and mother worked hard but did they did not earn much. Walter's clothes were hand-me-downs, passed from one family to another and kept for younger brothers and sisters. Meals were usually a thick vegetable soup, which was cooked in a black pot that hung over the fire. Rachel made flat barley bread, from barley that was really grown to feed the cattle. She was always pleased if Walter ma.   to collect some wild mushrooms, blackberries or nuts, s.   wede or turnip that had fallen off the back of a farm cart. Having some meat, an egg or a piece of cheese was a real treat.

Everyone in the family helped at haymaking time.

All through the summer the children had to collect dandelions and grass from the roadside to mix with the household scraps which the pig ate. They did not like it when the pig was killed late in the autumn, even though it meant they would have some roast meat, ham and bacon to eat.

Walter started school when he was five. Part of the school building that Walter knew is still in use today, but in his time there was only one big classroom and two teachers. Walter had a squeaky slate for writing on and he learnt to read by reciting sentences after the teacher. He had to learn lots of things off by heart, such as texts from the Bible and times tables.

Children of all ages were often taught together at school.

If the squire or his wife visited the school, one of the children had to stand up and recite something that he or she had learnt from memory. Sometimes the whole class had to sing to the visitors. Once a year an Inspector came to give the children a test. Those who did not pass were not allowed to go up to the next class.

However, life wasn't all hard work. Every May, Walter loved watching his dad march in the Friendly Society procession. The Society was a social club for working men and provided money for members when they were ill. It also paid for their funerals when they died. Every August, there was a church fête, with sack races for the children and other sports. Tea was laid out on long trestle tables and a brass band played while everyone ate.

In 1854, Walter was one of the first children to take a trip by train to the beach at Weymouth. He went with his Sunday School class soon after a new railway station was opened at Glastonbury. There was another treat every September when the Tor Fair was held in Glastonbury. The farmers took their animals to sell at the fair during the day, and in the evening there was a funfair with coconut shies and roundabouts.

When Walter was only seven, something terrible happened. His mother had a new baby boy but she died shortly after. Walter's father was left with four children, including a sickly new baby. The baby died too, five months after his mother.

Later that year Walter got a step-mother when his father married again. She was a servant girl called Caroline Martin.

When Walter grew up

Walter lived in Butleigh all his life. He left school when he was 12 and started work as a farm labourer like his father. We know he died when he was only 30 years old. Several other people in the village died at the same time, so perhaps they all died from the same illness.

Time line

National events

Personal events

1835 — Poor Law Act passed. New workhouses built.

1836 — Linton Workhouse opens with laundry, chapel and stables.

1837 — Queen Victoria becomes queen.

1838 — Queen Victoria's Coronation.

1845 — Butleigh National School opened.

1851 — Great Exhibition held at Crystal Palace in London.

1852 — Walter born.

1854 — Crimean War begins.

1856 — First rural police forces.

1863 — Sarah born.

1866 — Sarah's family moves to Linton Workhouse.

1870 — Education Act passed. All children to go to school.

1872 — Sarah's workhouse trip to the seaside.

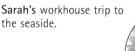

1873 — Agricultural Children's Act bans children under eight from working on farms.

1877 — First Canal Boat Act passed. Living conditions of boat families inspected for first time.

1878 — Richard born.

1880 — First steam boats on Leeds to Liverpool Canal. / Tommy and Eva born.

1881 — Richard's family found by census taker. Lanhydrock house destroyed by fire.

1887 — Queen Victoria's Golden Jubilee. / Tommy goes to boarding school in Reading.

1901 — Death of Queen Victoria.

How to find out more

Visit the local history collection in your library

Most libraries have collections of old newspapers, maps and census returns. All of these resources will help you to find out how people lived in your area during Victorian times. Compare what you find to how we live now.

Visit a museum

Go to your local museum and see if they have a section on how the people in your area lived during Victorian times.

Look round a village

The cottages, churches, chapels, and schools in most villages today were there in Victorian times. Look for clues such as houses called 'the old forge' or 'the old bakery'. See if any schools in the village have records dating back to the 19th Century.

Log on

Find out more about Victorian times on these websites.

www.nationaltrust.org.uk

Click on 'days out and visits', then 'find a place' and then 'a-z'. Click 'L' to find Lanhydrock. This is where Tommy and Eva lived. Click 'W' to find the work-house at Southwell in Nottinghamshire. Sarah and her family lived in a building like this.

www.workhouses.org.uk

You will find more information on workhouses on this site.

www.canaljunction.com

Click the box marked 'Canal Guides'. From the list under canal maps click 'Leeds to Liverpool'. You will be able to see modern photographs of the canal where Richard and his family lived.

www.somerset.gov.uk/somerset/culturecommunity/museums

Go to the site for the Somerset Rural Life Museum. This is where you will find a display about Walter's father, John Hodges.

Things to do

Write about your life

Write part of your autobiography. Illustrate it with drawings or photographs of you and the other people in your life. Add pictures of where you have lived and of important events that have happened since you were born. Include a map and a time line.

Write a Victorian biography

You only need to go back four generations to find people from your own family who were born in Queen Victoria's reign (1837-1901). Ask older relatives to write down the names of their grandparents and great grandparents. Ask where they lived, what jobs they did, and how many children they had. Ask if they have some old photographs of the family. Write all the information in a special notebook or on the computer, so that you can add to it when you find out more. Write a story about one of the people you have learnt about. Include a map and a time line, as well as pictures and photographs.

Imagine a conversation

Compare the experiences of two of the children in this book. Make up a conversation they might have had if they had met.

Become a researcher

Find out about the life of someone famous in Victorian times, such as Thomas Barnardo or Florence Nightingale. Or research the life of someone who lived in your area. Use reference books and search the internet. Can you find out anything about their childhood? How do their lives compare to those of the children in this book?

Reading list

The books listed below give an insight into country life in Victorian times. Look them up in your library.

Beatrix Potter, *The Tale of Peter Rabbit* and other titles by this famous Victorian storyteller and artist.
Alison Uttley, *A Country Child*. The autobiography of a well-known children's writer.
Geraldine Simonds, *The Workhouse Child*. A historic novel.

Places to visit

Lanhydrock, near Bodmin, Cornwall (01208 73320)
You can visit the house and see how and where Tommy and Eva lived. Find out about your nearest National Trust house from your local tourist office or by searching the National Trust website.

Visit a farming museum (01458 831197)
The Abbey Farm Museum in Glastonbury has an exhibition about John Hodges, Walter's father. You can visit any farm museum to see displays of tools, old photographs and displays about rural life.

The National Trust Workhouse, Southwell in Nottinghamshire (01636 817250)
Linton Workhouse, where Sarah lived, is now a Residential Home for the elderly. The National Trust has restored a workhouse in Southwell where you can see what Sarah's life may have been like.

The Boat Museum, Ellesmere Port, Cheshire (0151 3555017)
The National Waterways Museum, Gloucester Docks (01452 318054)
These museums give an insight into life on Britain's waterways in Victorian times.

Acknowledgements

Many thanks to Andrea Marchington and Mike England at Lanhydrock. The story of Walter is based on research done by Ann Healy of Butleigh and on the John Hodges display in the Abbey Museum, in Glastonbury. Siobhan Kirrane, former Museums Officer at the Craven Museum, Skipton, helped my initial research into Richard's story and directed me to the histories of the Leeds to Liverpool Canal. Linton Workhouse is now Symonds Residential Home. The Manager, Julia Nolan, was very helpful. Many thanks also to Mike Clarke for his photographs. Finally, many thanks to Chris Jakes from the Cambridgeshire Collection, for his help and for the photographs and reference material he provided.

Photographs: Somerset County Museum Service: 2, 24; The Family Records Centre: 5t, 12; Beamish. The North of England Open Air Museum. County Durham: 4t, 5m, 15t, 27, 28; Mike Clarke: 8, 9; The National Trust Workhouse Museum, Southwell, Nottinghamshire: 15b; The Cambridge Collection: 16; Lanhydrock: 19, 23; National Trust Photographic Library/Andreas von Einsiedel: 21. t=top; m=middle; b=bottom.

Index

This edition 2007
Published 2003 by A&C Black Publishers Limited
38 Soho Square, London W1D 3QZ
www.acblack.com

ISBN 978-0-7136-8825-2

Copyright text © Sallie Purkis, 2003
Copyright illustrations © Duncan Smith, 2003

A CIP record for this book is available from the British Library.

All rights reserved. No part of this publication may be reproduced in any form or by any means – graphic, electronic or mechanical, including photocopying, recording, taping or information storage and retrieval systems – without the prior permission in writing of the publishers.

Printed in Singapore by Tien Wah Press (Pte) Ltd

A&C Black uses paper produced with elemental chlorine-free pulp, harvested from managed sustainable forests.